To

_____

From

_____

_____

To Yasushi M.F.

Written and compiled by Sophie Piper
Illustrations copyright © 2007
Masumi Furukawa
This edition copyright © 2007 Lion Hudson

The moral rights of the author and
illustrator have been asserted

A Lion Children's Book
an imprint of
Lion Hudson plc
Wilkinson House, Jordan Hill Road,
Oxford OX2 8DR, England
www.lionhudson.com
ISBN 978 0 7459 6032 6

First edition 2007
This printing July 2009
10 9 8 7 6 5 4 3 2

A catalogue record for this book is available
from the British Library

Acknowledgments
All unattributed prayers are by Sophie
Piper and Lois Rock, copyright © Lion
Hudson. Prayers by Jenni Dutton and
Victoria Tebbs are copyright © Lion
Hudson.
Bible extracts are taken or adapted from the
Good News Bible, published by The Bible
Societies/HarperCollins Publishers Ltd, UK
© American Bible Society 1966, 1971,
1976, 1992, used by permission.
The Lord's Prayer (on page 54) from
Common Worship: Services and Prayers for
the Church of England (Church House
Publishing, 2000) is copyright © The
English Language Liturgical Consultation,
1988 and is reproduced by permission of the
publishers.

Typeset in 15/20 Goudy Old Style BT

Printed and bound in China
by Printplus Ltd

Prayers
for the
Very Young

Written and compiled by
Sophie Piper

Illustrated by
Masumi Furukawa

LION
CHILDREN'S

Contents

Morning
Prayers

Dearest God,
on this new day,
listen to me
as I pray.

Dearest God,
the day is new:
help me in
the things I do.

A Child of God

God, look down from heaven:
Here on earth you'll see
Someone looking upwards –
That someone is me.

Your sky is so big
and I am so small.
Never forget me,
never at all.

Here I am
in the great big world
with everywhere to explore;
and God made me
to live as his child
and love him for evermore.

Ready for the Day

I wake
I wash
I dress
I say:
'Thank you
God
for this
new day.'

Dear God,
What shall I wear today?
If I were dressing up like a guardian angel,
I would wear clean underwear and clean
outerwear and clean socks and clean shoes
and I would make sure I stayed clean all day;
except for mud and stuff, which even guardian
angels know don't really matter.

Growing Up Good

A little seed
unfolds its leaves
and grows up to the light;
and I will lift
my face to heaven
and learn to do what's right.

12

May my hands be helping hands
For all that must be done
That fetch and carry, lift and hold
And make the hard jobs fun.

May my hands be clever hands
In all I make and do
With sand and dough and clay
and things of paper, paint and glue.

May my hands be gentle hands
And may I never dare
To poke and prod and hurt and harm
But touch with love and care.

My Busy Day

This is a day for walking tall
This is a day for feeling small
This is a day for lots of noise
This is a day for quiet toys
This is a day to shout and sing
This is a day for everything.

Ready for sun
and ready for rain
and ready for all kinds of weather;
ready to hold
the hand of God
as we all go out together.

Family Prayers

Dear God, bless all my family,
as I tell you each name;
and please bless each one differently
for no one's quite the same.

Mummy and Me

Dear God,
When my mum is happy,
Let us laugh and play together.

When my mum is busy,
Let us do the work together.

When my mum is worried,
Let us sort things out together.

When my mum is weary,
Let us sit and rest together.

Dear God,
Take care of Mummy,
who takes good care of me,
and may our home be full of love
that all the world can see.

Dad

Bless my dad,
so strong and tall:
the kindest daddy
of them all.

God bless my daddy
through the bright blue day.
God bless my daddy
through the dark grey night.
God bless my daddy
when we hug together.
God bless my daddy
when he's out of sight.

My Big Family

Prayer number one is for baby
Prayer number two is for me
Prayer number three is for everyone
Who's part of my family tree.

Dear God,
Please take good care of me.
Take good care of my sister,
Take good care of my brother,
Take good care of those I love.
Take good care of those who love me.

Grans are good
and grans are fun.
Let us love them –
every one.

My Home

Dear Lord,
Please let our house be a home full of love –
a welcoming place for our family and friends.
May it be cosy and warm and light –
and brimming with laughter and joy.

Jenni Dutton

When the weather is cold
May our home be warm.

When the weather is wet
May our home be dry.

When the weather is hot
May our home give shade.

When the world is dark
May our home be bright.

For Our Food

Let us take a moment
To thank God for our food,
For friends around the table
And everything that's good.

The Lord is good to me,
And so I thank the Lord
For giving me the things I need,
The sun, the rain, the appleseed.
The Lord is good to me.

John Chapman, planter of orchards (1774–1845)

Prayers for a Wonderful World

Thank you, dear God,
for the deep brown earth
and the shimmering sea so green.

Thank you, dear God,
for the high blue sky
and the wind that blows all unseen.

For the Seasons

Thank you for spring
and the waking time.

Thank you for summer
and the growing time.

Thank you for autumn
and the gathering time.

Thank you for winter
and the resting time.

The sun may shine
The rain may fall
God will always
Love us all.

Victoria Tebbs

31

For Little Creatures

He prayeth best, who loveth best
All things both great and small;
For the dear God who loveth us,
He made and loveth all.

S. T. Coleridge (1772–1834)

The little bugs that scurry,
The little beasts that creep
Among the grasses and the weeds
And where the leaves are deep:
All of them were made by God
As part of God's design.
Remember that the world is theirs,
Not only yours and mine.

For Amazing Animals

Bless the hungry lion and its ROAR
Bless the big brown bear and its GROWL
Bless the sly hyena and its scary HA HA HA
Bless the wolves who see the moon and
    HOWL!

Multicoloured animals
With stripes and dots and patches:
God made each one different –
There isn't one that matches.

Prayers for Special Days

God, please take great care of us
on this, our special day.
Please, God, send the golden sun
and blow the rain away.

May we all stay very safe,
and may we all have fun.
Now we have to hurry, God,
our great day has begun.

Birthdays

Thank you for the year gone by
and all that I have done.
Thank you for my birthday
and the year that is to come.

Bless my hair and bless
my toes
Bless my ears and bless
my nose
Bless my eyes and bless
each hand
Bless the feet on which
I stand
Bless my elbows, bless
each knee:
God bless every part
of me.

Holidays

Our journey may be fast
Our journey may be slow
May God be always with us
Wherever we may go.

I love to have sand between my toes,
to watch the tide as it comes and goes,
to pick up shells and throw them away:
thank you, dear God, for my holiday.

Christmas

Let us travel to Christmas
By the light of a star.
Let us go to the hillside
Right where the shepherds are.
Let us see shining angels
Singing from heaven above.
Let us see Mary cradling
God's holy child with love.

Christmas candle, golden fire,
in the darkest night;
Jesus, help me follow you;
make my whole world bright.

Easter

In the Easter garden
the leaves are turning green;
in the Easter garden
the risen Lord is seen.

In the Easter garden
we know that God above
brings us all to heaven
through Jesus and his love.

I am laughing 'cos of spring,
Laughing 'cos of everything,
Laughing yellow, laughing blue,
Laughing 'cos of me and you,
Laughing blossom, laughing pink –
God is laughing too, I think.

Harvest

The harvests have ripened in the sun;
There's plenty of food for everyone:
There's some for ourselves and more to share
With all of God's people everywhere.

The harvest of our garden
is astonishingly small;
but oh, dear God, we thank you
that there's anything at all.

Prayers for Quiet Times

Help us to remember
All your love and care,
Trust in you and love you,
Always, everywhere.

W. St Hill Bourne (1846–1929)

Feeling Sorry

The wrong I have done
now makes me sad;
The love that God gives
will make me glad.

Take away the wrong I did
and throw it far away
Help me to be brave and strong
and start a bright new day.

Feeling Sad

Dear God,
This is a sad day.
This is a day filled
   with tears.
This is the sort of day that only you can mend,
   dear God.
Please come and make things better.

Dear God, you are my shepherd,
You give me all I need,
You take me where the grass grows green
And I can safely feed.

You take me where the water
Is quiet and cool and clear;
And there I rest and know I'm safe
For you are always near.

From Psalm 23

Learning to Pray

I'm standing here upon the earth
and looking to the sky.
I'm trusting that my quiet prayers
can reach to God on high.

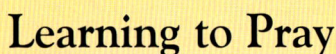

Our Father in heaven,
hallowed be your name,
your kingdom come,
your will be done,
on earth as in heaven.
Give us today our daily bread.
Forgive us our sins
as we forgive those who sin against us.
Lead us not into temptation
but deliver us from evil.
For the kingdom, the power,
and the glory are yours
now and for ever.
Amen

The Lord's Prayer

Blessings

Bless the day, dear God,
from sunrise to sunset.
Bless the night, dear God,
from sunset to sunrise.

Goodbyes

Dear God,
Bless us each and every one.
Bless our time together.
Bless us as we say goodbye.
Bless us as we go on our way
and keep us safe.
Amen

Goodbye to all that's been;
Hello to what will be;
God bless us each and every one,
God bless you, God bless me.

Goodnight

Lord, keep us safe this night,
Secure from all our fears;
May angels guard us while we sleep,
Till morning light appears.

John Leland (1754–1841)

Now I lay me down to sleep,
I pray thee, Lord, thy child to keep;
Thy love to guard me through the night
And wake me in the morning light.

Traditional

Index of First Lines

The moon shines bright,
The stars give light
Before the break of day;
God bless you all
Both great and small
And send a joyful day.

Traditional